KENTUCKY DERBY

Andrea Cohen

To Nick —
With all Best
Wishes
— Ahn

salmonpoetry

Published in 2011 by
Salmon Poetry
Cliffs of Moher, County Clare, Ireland
Website: www.salmonpoetry.com
Email: info@salmonpoetry.com

ISBN 978-1-907056-56-7 PB / 978-907056-66-6 HB

Typesetting: *Siobhán Hutson*
Cover design: *Robin Ratcliff at Fyfe Design*

For my mother

To make a prairie it takes a clover and one bee,
One clover, and a bee.
And revery.
The revery alone will do,
If bees are few.

—EMILY DICKINSON

Acknowledgements

I am grateful to the editors of these journals, in which the following poems appeared, sometimes in slightly different incarnations.

Ancora Impara: "Self Portrait with the Cinnabons"
Bark: "Seven Dogs"
The Cincinnati Review: "Elegy for the Nail"
Dark Sky Magazine: "Tragicomedy"
Diode: "Self Portrait with Forgiveness," "English as a Second Language"
The Hudson Review: "Jell-O," "Transport," "Hope is Dead"
Journal of Family Life: "22-Foot Mother"
The Manhattan Review: "Self Mailer," "Basement," "Self Portrait as Fourth Fate," "Chicken, Airplane, Soldier," "Person as a Substitute for Two People," "Ripple," "Coupons in the Afterlife," "Self Portrait with Chain Saw," "Three-Legged Race," "Reverse Egg Hunt," "The Gates of Paradise"
Memorious: "Live Girls"
The Morning News: "Kentucky Derby"
Orion: "After Reading Juarroz"
Poetry: "Butter," "To Whom It May Concern," "Petition"
Provincetown Arts: "To the Lifeboats"
Salamander: "Rolling and Walking," "Self Diagnosis and Treatment," "Home is Where"
The Threepenny Review: "Hardtack"
Tuesday: "Found in Translation"
Vinyl: "Explication of Text," "Garnish," "Annulment"
White Whale Review: "As Balthus Did"

"22-Foot Mother" appears in *Full of Grace,* by Judith Dupré (Random House, 2010)

"Seven Dogs" appears in *Dogs Singing – A Tribute Anthology*, edited by Jessie Lendennie (Salmon Poetry, 2010)

Peppermints to Gail Caldwell, Amy Anderson, Giavanna Munafo, Tom Sleigh, Joyce Peseroff, Rebecca Morgan Frank, Mary Bisbee-Beek, Jessie Lendennie, Siobhán Hutson, and my family.

For above-and-beyondness, carrots to Anna Schuleit, sugar cubes to Francesca Bewer, and one unending victory lap to The MacDowell Colony.

Contents

To Whom It May Concern

for Harry Cobb

Soon I'll move to Norway.
If that's a bitter pill,

well, swill, swallow. I'm going,
and I won't wallow, not in Norway,

where they're so beyond
slave labor, with laws that say

a clerk must work within five
meters of a window through

which she can see a tree
and by that tree by seen.

My mind's made up.
I will be Norwegian with Norwegian

trees. I'll be seer and be seen.
It's a scenic scene, it's

how it goes, I'm going.
Tell the top brass, if

they ask, I don't give
a damn about their asses.

But I will miss the beeches and the ashes.
It's not their fault I'm leaving.

They're only trees, and
leaving, I'm Norwegian.

Butter

I've never seen the land
of milk and honey, but once,

at the Iowa State Fair, I glimpsed
a cow fashioned of butter.

It lived behind a window
in an icy room, beneath klieg lights.

I filed past as one files
past a casket at a wake.

It was that sad: a butter cow
without a butter calf. Nearby I spied

a butter motorcycle, motorcycle-
sized, a mechanical afterthought

I thought the cow might have liked to ride.
You don't drive a motorcycle; you ride it.

But not if you're a butter cow, not
if you're a butter cow who's seen, if

not the land of milk and honey, the land
of milk, and dwelled within it.

It had a short life span, the butter cow.
Before it died, I looked

deep into its butter eyes. It saw
my butter soul. I could

have wept, or spread myself,
for nobody, across dry toast.

Petition

after Elinor Lipper

The creature that had once
been a man handed over his petition,
a stained and grimy scrap,
handed it to his lord and master,
a petition asking to be transferred
to the status of a horse.
You son-of-a-whore, the master,
kicking for good measure, bellowed.
What do you mean by this?
The creature that had once
been a man, having considered
deeply his petition, answered:
If I were a horse, I would have
one day off in ten. As is,
I have none. As a horse,
I could rest now and again
during work. As a former
man, I cannot. As a horse,
I would be expected to perform
work equal to my strength.
As a prisoner, I am always
hungry, and hungry, I
work less and get less
bread, so I can barely stand.
A horse gets a stable
and two blankets. I have
no blankets, no jacket.
If a driver beats
a horse too hard, he
is punished, for a horse
is precious. If the brigadiers
beat and kick me, it is like

beating a tree. So you see,
a prisoner is nothing here.
But a horse?
A horse is something!
Inside the frozen
and the broken
vista, the plea had a ring
of truth heard
even by the lord
and master, who had
himself once been a man,
and who, when no other
former men could see,
attached that name
to the page, granting
the horse a stable and two blankets.

Rolling and Walking

Let's be clear: some
of the walking wounded
are confined to chairs.
Their hairdos, like
the past and future,
are elements somewhat
beyond their control.
One woman shows
how the chair
goes forward and back
by virtue of her breath,
directed. She says:
they don't call it
the suck and blow
chair because that sounds
pornographic. She sucks
and blows, turns three
tight circles, and out
of breath, laughs:
those are my moves.
Her moves are in
her head too, where
she dreams she's walking,
pursuing her chair.
She was asleep
when the accident happened.
She remembers a man
reaching in through the pick-up's
smashed back window to hold
her head in place. It was
her neck that had broken.
But her head was clear, she
was awake, she closed
her eyes to keep dust out.

There was a lot
of dust. Some was settling.
Some people in another
vehicle were already dust
or about to become it.
She could hear sirens, which
she took as a good sign:
help was near and she could hear.
A siren on an otherwise
bright day when your boyfriend falls
asleep can mean disaster or all clear.
It matters if he's at the wheel
of a truck, or turning over after love.
Sometimes we hear glass
breaking, sometimes our own
bones. Sometimes you can't know
what you hear or don't,
what ringing's real or in your head.
She tells of going to Sea World
now, how it's different: *I still love
the seals and whales*, she says, *but I
don't get tired. At the end of the day,
people on their feet, they feel
fatigue. I forget about their troubles.*
Studies of lottery winners suggest
people are roughly as happy
before as they are after.
She said to her parents
in intensive care: *Aren't we lucky
to meet so many nice folks?*
We're walking or rolling
through Sea World, through stop
signs, through the Valley of Death.
We can suck and blow.
We keep going.
That's all I know.

Jell-O

O, I remember those days
stuck in bed with a lunch
that wiggled, like a pet
that happy to see you,
a pet you were meant to eat.
O, you felt wretched.
At Morrison's Cafeteria, Jell-O
came in yellow, green and bright
red squares, like sawed blocks
of ice that couldn't sit still,
like the horses' hooves
they were, still racing
around the track, or running
from the handler about to hand
one over to the man
who stopped there once a month.
He would have had a scent
of death the horses would
have bucked at, would have
feared like death. That was what
my mother, who loved me,
served me up when I was sick.
O, love is strange, we do
strange things: give a child
a wild-eyed herd of horses
in a bowl and expect
her to get better.

Self Mailer

In the old days you could mail
yourself to Marblehead, Mass.,
with just your name, the town,

and a stamp, although COD was possible
too, so that when you arrived
at your address, you could inspect

your contents, see which parts
of you had broken, whether
the breaks were minor or worth fixing.

You could decide to pay up
or send yourself back.
This was long ago. We called it

the past, which came with some
fanfare in a steamer trunk
and seemed so simple.

Self Portrait with Forgiveness

Maybe forgiveness could take
the shape of a fish

I place in the heel
of a clear, plastic shoe

filled with water.
There would be one

fish in each shoe. They
would be in love—

with each other, not me—
but eternally divided.

They would be brilliant
and orange and I

would walk around on them
all day and every night

they'd tuck me in,
repeating: it's alright, it's alright.

Self Portrait as Fourth Fate

I'm the black sheep
of the fates, all sun
and light, the sister
the myths forget
to mention. I'm
the youngest, not Clotho.
I questioned, I rebelled,
beginning with free love
and graduating to teach
free will at the community college.
I believe you get to choose,
I yell from my soap box
on 6th Avenue. *I believe in self-
determination*, I bellow
as Atropos passes
with her sharp glance.
I tell Clotho: *Save yourself,
ditch that lousy spinner.*
And to Lacheris, with teddy bear
of tape measure: *It's not too late.*
They could get vocational
training, make a useful contribution.
I believe this. I believe
even fates can change.
Look at me, I plead
with my oldest sister, waking
to her kneeling over me
with that old saw. A saw
with teeth, and she
pretends not to see,
not to hear my entreaty:
Sister, Atropos, it's me.

Person as a Substitute for Two People

That's a lot to ask
of one person: that
she stand in for twice
the number of legs,
noses, etc. But
we do, asking, *Will you?*
My love promises
to make biscuits
the way Colette did,
to tango as Alexis
swore only she could.
To say the one
you choose is a substitute
for two is to put it
mildly. I'm a three-
ring circus, still learning
to ride bareback
without a horse.
Love demands that.
Love demands that the high
wire double as net.
We're all working overtime here,
in clown suit, in top
hat, taking tickets while placing
our heads inside the mouths
of the big cats we are.
We're playing for the crowd
of one, for the kid who thought
the trick impossible. Look:
no hands, and then, many
hands where there were none.

To the Lifeboats

To the lifeboats, says the sign, in Portuguese
and Spanish above the door leading
to the deck, leading to the sea
from the dinner table overflowing at Bob and Lise's,
post-sunset, with Portuguese stew and a Spanish
Flamenco dancer everybody wants to bed,
with cursing and affection in fourteen languages,
with magnums of red wine that disappear
and re-appear, with a toast to Long Point,
whose flashing green beacon keeps the lovesick
ferry captain from crashing into the breakwater.
In attendance, we've got a Buddhist torch singer
channeling Edith Piaf and Bob Dylan,
we've got our own Bob crooning the ghostly, atonal
suicide ditty his mother fed him as a boy, we've got
the retired coastal geologist explaining
that the spit of land we're perched on
is fast eroding, washing away, which heats
things up, so someone opens a window,
admitting our frailty, admitting the sea
breeze, and the Flamenco dancer shows
us a polka, whispering, *that's my secret
pleasure*, and the recent widow grieves
briefly behind her blue sleeve, then rejoins
the festivities. In the end, we have the beginning
and the end and the whole unraveling in between.
We have the nearly full moon
rising, orange and pocked like a Fiesta Ware
plate floated up from a ghost ship. We've got
the tide coming in, the specter of undressing
for the ritual midnight swim. We've got the geologist
repeating his science lesson, the melting hand-
churned cherry ice cream his prop, and we
all see the writing on the wall:

Alos botes salvavidas
Para os botes salva-vidas,
directions to the lifeboats
in Spanish and Portuguese, the sign's elegant
steel lettering the one memento a daughter
salvaged from her father's sinking ship.
Forget what the sign says, we're all
going down—in the ship, in the lifeboats,
in the manse beside the sea. But now
we're up to our ears in singing, and the shy
puppeteer pipes up to ask: *that fable*
about the needle, that's about
true love, isn't it? And even
those of us who don't know the story,
who have no idea what she's talking
about, nod in agreement, thinking about
what we stitch so clumsily together, about the needle's
prick, like that of the beach rose stem, the rosa
rugosa that grows everywhere here. We nod as those
blooms nod in high wind, because the only
story worth telling, whether you're selling
lifeboats or needles or soup with linguica,
is about true love, right? Why
else guffaw or go teary as the ship
goes down, as the sliver of land in this ever-
shifting light show slips from us, if not, amiga,
amigo, for the salt-sting of true-blue love?

Ripple

My friend and I sit
inside an orbit of black
flies by the lake. She
is teaching me to meditate,
how to concentrate on breath
entering and exiting.
I am concentrating on her lips.
They breathe and speak about breathing.
I am concentrating on the halo
of black flies whose welt bites
can take a day to surface.
It can take decades for the effects
of one late spring afternoon
by an otherwise unpeopled lake
to reveal themselves. We are discussing
the amazing properties of
water. What is it? she asks.
Hydrogen and oxygen, I say,
though I believe she's after
a less scientific explanation, some
metaphor elucidating displacement.
When she places her left foot
in the lake, the water envelopes
it as curious minnows might.
When you enter into
anything, there are consequences.
A rise in lake level, ripples.
Some seen, some felt.
Some imperceptible, like unseen
layers, an invisible surround-gown
of armor we are meaning,
on this momentary
quay, to step out of—

Found in Translation

We were in the weeds, up
to our necks in customers needing miso

soup, sushi, and colder Kirins and I
was trying to explain an expression

to Yasuyo, the diminutive hostess
whose husband owned Hello Sushi and

was cozied in at the bar, smoking Silk Cuts
and slurping uni and saki with

his girlfriend decked out in an emerald
silk dress. I was trying to explain

the expression: like a chicken
with its head cut off. There was much

running around, a lot of going
on automatic pilot, pretending the customer

was always right. By the end
of the night, when everyone

but the husband and his mistress
had left, Yasuyo turned to me

and said: I get the chicken. She said it
with her lips, which were set

firmly in her head. The rest
of her had already fled.

I Will Not . . .

I don't recollect
the rest of the sentence,
only that I was made

to write it one hundred times
for the tyrant Mrs. Udinsky,
the Sunday school teacher who

addressed me as *Madame You
Will Not* and whose gravel
heart would have been glad

to hear how I bawled all
Saturday night in anticipation
of her wrath, a rancor as unstoppable

as my cramped hand
across that page, the hand that wrote
one hundred times for Mrs. Udinsky:

I will not, I will not, and then,
for me, threefold:
I will, I will, I will . . .

Three-Legged Race

The sum is less
than the parts,
if you're counting
the bound inner legs
of two kids as one.
But the three-legged race
demands its own
accounting: the sacrifice
of speed and grace
for the clumsiness
of companionship,
a race that lets children
ape the long-
married—those distance
athletes who've learned
by trial and error
to breathe deeply
and uniquely, to move
together, to keep arms
fast around the other, to
adjust to a partner's speed
or distraction, and as
importantly, when falling,
to laugh at the inside
joke of it, to gape at the huge
blue or bleary canopy,
to struggle upwards
and hop along, oblivious
to the cheers, to the ribbons
and pennants awarded the so-
called victors stumbling
across the finish.

The Universal Truth

My friend, the secrets
of the universe are trying
on new disguises.
At thirteen I dressed
like a bent, old woman,
with fake, sagged breasts,
powdered hair and spectacles
through which I stared
at the 5 & Dime straight
into my mother's eyes.
She stared straight back,
not seeing me
as she fingered the felt
pipe cleaners and moustache
trimmers. My father did not
smoke, was clean-shaven.
The bearded, smoking gun
would have been the discrete
and dashing Mr. Peters
down the street,
and my mother—blushing,
furtive, unrecognizable—
would have been
the stranger
I was becoming.

Coupons in the Afterlife

I accept that generally speaking
we're required to check
our stuff at the door,
but I'm requesting a special
dispensation for coupons, those
scissored IOUs as yet uncashed.
I'm not asking for the doubling
of face value—even the Piggly Wiggly
gave up on that, but 10 cents off
on English muffins—how hard could that be?
I love my nooks and crannies,
those shallow labyrinths a child
can devour, and why not
reward frugality? My mother, who could
afford not to, clipped constantly,
cutting the heart out of any
back story: flood, double shooting,
space travel. Maybe she knew
what I don't: that you can
take them with you, that even
if you can't spend the coupons,
you can arrange them
in the afterlife, in simple frames,
snapshots of the old country, land
of appetite and the hand that feeds you
at a discount, homeland from which
the dearly beloved, in steerage,
in a rickety ship, are sailing now.

Elegy for the Nail

So you get hammered
going in, you get

bent. Forget about it.
Forget your princely

carriage when first forged.
So you've lived

a little, so you hold
two pieces of a tired

door in place, or better,
the scent of my secret

love's sweater.

Seven Dogs

The life of a man
is measured by seven dogs.

The first dog says: and now
we shall eat and lap

water and walk in the woods.
We will sleep often in sunny spots.

There will be much
chasing of squirrels, but we

will not speak of death.
Then the man speaks

of death to himself, but
not to the second dog, who

must learn to heel
and come, and this goes

on. Seven dogs. And then one
evening the seven dogs

come to him with seven
sets of slippers. It's a trick

they never mastered in life.
Is it time? he asks. And

he follows his pack, good
dog that he is, into the woods.

Reverse Egg Hunt

In this version
you hide
from the eggs.

This version requires
a new kind
of patience.

The eggs have no
intention of finding you.
They're not even looking.

This is the game
you've been playing
all along, without knowing.

Vertical Poem

after Juarroz

The white road,
birch-like, turns.
I am happy
to observe
its path
between green hills.
It is full
of promise.
One must step
lightly on such
a road, and
from a distance.

Not an Antidote

When I came
unawares upon the buck
I stopped dead
in my tracks, seeing
his dead eye
eye-level, hung
as he was, upside
down by his trussed
hind legs from the oak
I can't pass now
without the scent
of life inverted.

Blake tells me
of a fawn he saw
curled up in sun
beside the cottage
all day, so still
he was afraid,
but come evening,
its mother came
to fetch it:
not an antidote,
but a doe the mind
makes permanent.

As Balthus Did

Where are we? I ask.
We're driving in a boat
of an old, golden Buick
convertible, beside a slide
show of rippling lake.
We're in a place
in the world, my friend says.
This is good to know.
I'm ignoring the road.
My friend, who is driving,
is also ignoring the road
somewhat, veering off as we talk.
We talk the way you can
in a foreign land, where
other people are white noise.
But we're here, high and deep
in New England, in a sort of period
piece with saw mill and grist mill,
with the requisite river on which
the brick library appears
to be floating. Given
its exposure, this spot took
the hit when the ice storm blew in.
Birches fly at half mast now,
their upper reaches hanging
kamikaze-like above the blacktop.
I'm feeling high and raw and
dangerous myself, confessing my bliss
as we drift past sheep, past lambs,
past the herd dog whose bark
asks: friend or foe? Friend, my friend,
friend. Near Cold Comfort Farm
we steer into the woods and find
a stash of fossilized beer cans

that may have fueled a talk
like ours fifty years back.
The vessels are crumbling, rusted,
seductive, empty only in
the conventional sense. We gather
them as we would exquisitely
plumed and injured birds.
My friend says she'd like to live
with the animals, as Balthus did.
She'd like to convert the garage
into a mews, to bring the horses
into the house. They'd be
a source of heat and part
of the family. There's ample
logic there, and beyond: imagine
dreaming in that saddle bed
above those hooves, galloping
anywhere and everywhere
in the world, and waking here.

After Reading Juarroz

All day the tree
has been falling
from its fruit.

The sound is terrible.

It's the part even
hardened reporters
leave out of stories.

The fruits roll
into the ditch.

Even the wind,
even the flies,
in their sorrow,

will not touch them.

Gaucin, Dusk

The sheep
            down

      the green hill

                  arrange

                              and   rearrange

                        themselves

                  like   a   ruin

trying

            to   get

                                          comfortable

Hollow

The nest I found
in that mowed meadow

I brought home, thinking
it tree-tumbled.

I did not know
some deft birds build

close to the ground.
I did not know

the heart I found
beating in a stream

had been squirreled
there for safe keeping.

I brought it home.
I placed it in the nest,

where, soon, by virtue
of its murmurings, I realized

it was mine. How heart-
breaking those cries,

what heaviness
as I carried that bleating

thing through deep woods
back to that cold stream.

Basement

He liked to fix things, he
liked to tinker. He sat on the edge
of his daughter's childhood

bed, his lap a snake pit
of broken wristwatches,
his fly unzipped.

He said, if you two stick
—meaning his daughter and me—
I'll give you one of these.

Meaning one of the watches, fixed.
She didn't say exactly
what had happened

down there, but when
he started in
on her sister, she blew

the whistle. He did some time:
three months, after which
the prison guard dropped by

for beers and smokes.
They'd hang out
in the basement, where

he liked to carve
duck decoys, where he took
things apart to see

how they worked
or didn't. The basement
was filled with antique clocks.

They ticked like clockwork.
His daughter and I
didn't stick: he was better

at breaking than mending, and she
was beautiful, broken, and his.

Live Girls

That's an exaggeration.
There's only one live girl
upstairs, and she barely moves.
Instead, the students move
around her in the life
drawing class, dragging their easels,
so from downstairs it sounds
like children pulling heavy
wagons without wheels. Downstairs,
the invited luminary is trying
to recite poetry about death,
but constantly stopping because
of the screeching of easels
from above, which may remind
her of fingernails on a chalkboard,
of an episode when the class clown
erased her sonnet from the board—
a piece about a dying horse
which the young poet sensed,
even then, formed the germ of her oeuvre.
But this is conjecture, and further
distraction from the luminary
now darkening the stage, the fright
wig she is above the podium growing
more frightening as she glares
up at the ceiling, as if
her wrath could bring it down.
She does not bring down the house.
Her arsenal includes death and more death—
child's play compared with the live girl
upstairs, the girl with fleshy folds, nose
ring, a lizard tattoo you'd swear
not fit for refrigerator art but which, on her,
becomes unspeakably alluring, as the students,

circling, edge nearer, the way two newlywed
brides, holding hands and cell phone
cameras, having driven all night from Nice
to Paris, advance on the Mona Lisa.
Like us, they've heard:
come close enough to the bullet-
proof glass and you can see her
breath fogging the case's interior.
You can take a picture of it.
But this is a case of mistakenly
talking about the Mona Lisa
and French brides and the live
girl in lieu of focusing
on the famous poet, who abhors
distraction, unless it involves looking
away from the wan vase of irises into her own
eyes, which are watering as they recite
her swan song of irises, a bouquet
she's slaughtered by merest mention.
Meanwhile, the live girl scratches
her nose, the teacher closes
the window (more noise), and the Monday
night class advances its easels in a circular
fashion around her, the way the restaurant
atop the Hyatt Regency rotated beneath
its blue glass dome in '67, when that blue
dome was the Atlanta skyline, before a whole
glass forest grew up around it. This too
is a diversion, but my father took me there,
to lunch at the Polaris, decades before we'd ever
taste loss, and I'd like to take you there,
to where I placed a sugar packet
on the ledge at the edge of the table,
and after an hour of oyster Po-boys, Coca-Colas,
Take the "A" Train, and a dizzying
vista, the table had returned
to that packet. I want to believe

we're on a journey that returns us
to sweetness. I want to believe that when
the famous poet insists she will never
read here again, she means it. This
is a humble venue, painted a deep,
strange green and she cannot compete
with the ruckus even one live girl,
barely moving, makes, as even now,
after the girl's left the room
for a cigarette break in a blue
kimono, the students close their eyes,
re-position their easels and try,
with charcoal stubs,
to approximate that glowing.

Tragicomedy

Jean-Jacques, an outcast
from the Comédie Française,
taught me to say
je t'aime convincingly
in a little theater
near the Seine.
He demonstrated,
while reciting
the line, how
to pick invisible
lint from the sleeve
of a sweater.
It didn't matter
whose sweater,
whether solid
or argyle, whether
the object of make-
believe ardor responded.
This was beginner's
acting in a foreign tongue.
I studied hard, harnessed
my wits to pick
girls up by the river,
by the bucketful.
I'm picking lint
as fast as I
can, as fast
as jilted girls
can toss themselves
into the Seine.
Je t'aime,
quand même.

Chicken, Airplane, Soldier

Chicken, airplane, soldier,
the swim instructor, standing waist-
high in the town pool, repeats
to his pupil, a boy accustomed
to thrashing on land, who's
floating on his back now, face
screwed in concentration, body
cruising backwards by virtue of taking
dictation: chicken, airplane, soldier—
meaning, arms bent like chicken
wings, then extended like wings
of a plane, then flush at his sides
like the arms of soldiers (who
don't have wings). The trick
is speaking to the boy in a tongue
he understands, one that gives
permission to shift seamlessly
between animal, man-made, and man,
to glimpse the possibilities that might
follow boyhood while his eyes
follow the ceiling tiles, counting
compulsively because his mind takes
stock, taking into account how many
chickens and airplanes and soldiers
he gets to be lurching the backwards
length of the pool. It's the elementary
backstroke, a style not found
in competition, but recommended
for survival, say, if your ship,
coming in, should sink. This style
lets you glide until land or a life-
boat approaches. It's a stroke
that encourages cloud study, by
which the resourceful boy finds
what he needs in thin air and—chicken,
airplane, soldier—in himself.

Home is Where

When Barbara Bachman invited me next door
for dinner, she was made to recite the menu, which

wasn't impolite, but Darwinian. Spaghetti trumps rump
roast trumps fish. Some parents built rec rooms

to attract kids, with pinball, ping pong, the industrial
popcorn popper. Our mother was practical,

thinking big picture, long term, converting
our basement into a swank bomb shelter

with beluga and smoked oysters for grown-ups,
chocolate turtles and cheese puffs for kids.

We had jars of cling peaches in syrup,
bourbon, Bing cherries, Lucky Strikes

on silver platters. The pièce de résistance
was the sound system my father rigged up,

with Swedish speakers and killer amp
linked to his reel-to-reel of canned laughter.

It was the odd Saturday night when
everybody we knew didn't crowd in

for an emergency drill, swilling
oysters and booze to that music, imagining

the earth taking its final curtsy, and us
so giddy we were miles beyond the punch

line, ecstatic, laughing along
until the sweet, sweet end.

First Death in New York, 1967

I understood that people dressed formally for god and airplanes. I knew that New York was a city in the north, that its skyscrapers were built especially to cast endless shadows over men with masks and knives and desires. I comprehended that these men desired things they didn't have, like my mother's red purse with the golden clasp and wintergreen mints inside. I wasn't sure what might be longer: a building's shadow or the blade of a knife. I didn't know how many times a person could die, so each day that she was gone, I buried myself in her closet with the sheer nightgown that smelled less and less of her and more of my going on without her.

Self Diagnosis and Treatment

For mild tremors, no treatment
is needed. If tremors
persist, these simple measures

may help: grasping objects firmly,
holding them close to the body
without dropping, avoiding

uncomfortable positions, not eating
soup in public, using utensils
with large handles, including

butter hooks, spittoons, and shoe horns.
Drinking alcohol in moderation
may lessen the tremor

or make it worse.
Simply holding on
to a person with a more

persistent tremor may provide
some relief. In rare instances,
those with tremors in locations

prone to earthquakes may find
their tremors, if persisting,
less apparent, less troubling.

English as a Second Language

He studied hard. He
was small and quick, like
a minnow swimming.

He liked the idioms
in English, especially
phrases like: I left

the past behind me,
the glass half full.
After class he asked:

what is the word
for the sound a knife
makes entering flesh?

Is it different for flesh
very young or old?
What is the word

that means to hold
a fish? I held him
briefly. His scars darted

in and out and then
we were water
under the bridge.

Hardtack

Call it what you will—
sea or ship or pilot's biscuit—
either way it's flour and water,
a tasteless concoction a sailor
stacks like poker chips
inside his cap and then devours
as if, storm- and wave-
tossed on the high seas,
he were the high-stakes
game he hoped to win.
When you're a sailor, starving,
existing on a staple of saltless
hardtack, when all you can see
is a sea of salt, the salt
of other men, or in the blistering
wind, the salt of your own tears,
there's little to win.
You bite your tongue
when the captain hurls
another insult, when he unfurls
the tip of his dark whip.
You bite down hard
on the hardtack, pretending
it's his hand, which doesn't
feed you. You bite down
on the weevils and the mold
inherent in hardtack, in the cracker
as hard as the hold where, exhausted,
you fall between your hard and salt-
caked mates, each in his own
despair, each in his own self-
remedying dream: the scent of earth,
urgent, continents from salt-stung air.

What You Missed

for S.D.

We had canned soup
for dinner last night.
It had some kind
of potatoes and taste.
After that, the dog
and I navigated black ice.
This involved sliding,
falling, getting up.
Everyone I know
slid, fell, got up.
But not you.
You were dead
by your own hand.
What was that
hand thinking?
Did it shake,
did it hope
another hand
would grapple with it?
We had canned soup
for dinner last night.
There may have been
some stars above
the snow-cold woods.
One may have glistened
the way a white
bowl will, placed
on the wooden
table, out of
habit, for one
who's missing.

Elf Portrait

The s went
on holiday, leaving
the essence
of me: a small
working stiff
bent over a
workbench,
attaching wheels
to trucks,
hammering rails
for toy train sets.
I missed my
grander self, who eschewed
hard labor, who
gazed eons
into mirrors.
Then Boxing Day
came and overnight
the shop closed shop.
No thank you, no
severance. I hit
the road. I
roamed, ate sometimes
from a can,
sometimes the can itself.
Untethered, unmoored,
I found my elfin
self gaining momentum,
and not in a good
way, barreling down a one-
lane highway, a plunging
frame of mind that would
have been the scenic end
of me had I not glanced

and seen the s
rain–swept, shivering,
flying solo, not
reclining, but sideways
on a yellow sign, alerting
me to the swerve ahead.
That's the self–
sacrifice that saved
this elf.

Self Portrait with Chain Saw

Along with me and the chain saw,
there's my fear of the chain saw,
and my certainty that it navigates
in one direction: toward me.
Additionally, there's the chain saw's appetite
for big sky, for dividing
whatever thinks it can't
be halved, and there's the fresh
memory of Lucy H. sculpting
in her fourth-floor loft, with sketches, with
deadlines, with a chain saw that
kicks back, hitting her in the chest,
missing the jugular, but nicking other vital
items, blood coming fast and Lucy managing
to dial 911, whose operator demands
she name the man who did this,
and Lucy stammering, *it was an accident,*
five times before dragging
her way downstairs, out the door
to the corner where she collapses,
where the man who sells oranges and pears
on 3rd Avenue, not caring who's to blame—
random sad sack or chain saw or Lucy's
own misguided hand—picks her up
and runs, carrying her until a speeding cab
stops and speeds them to the nearest ER,
where she survives to plan
a performance piece without audience:
the saw's proper burial at sea.
So you see, no self portrait
with a chain saw is complete
without Lucy, without the thick-headed,
well-meaning operator, without the good
Samaritan green grocer, without

the cab driver who knew all the shortcuts
and took them, without the surgeon
who sewed as nimbly
as the chain saw cut, without
the good and the bad and the dumb
luck of it all, without the sea and its bit
part, without me, without the chain
saw, which, for all its dividing unites.

Edge

Easy, at lake's
edge, you and the water
clear and lilac-fringed, to call
it paradise, to imagine
yourself, happy, happily
immersed. And then a black
snake shakes the shallows,
its slither triggering
a fear primeval. You say:
each of us dreads one thing
enough to betray all
we love, meaning a thing
that can unmake us.
Maybe, but friend, we could
instead step back
from this edge,
onto the Navajo rug.
One unmatched thread
runs to its edge,
an intentional flaw meant
to free the weaving's life
force for future incarnations.
They call it the spirit line.
It resembles a carefully
placed snake. Imagine a snake
shedding its skin, a snake
shaking off sin. Imagine a vista
unfalling, unfallen. Imagine standing
by that lake, imagine diving
into it, the imperfect and authentic
thread our bodies make
a spirit trope—as in turning toward—
each other and the other shore.

Hope is Dead

Hope is dead, he said,
meaning his botanist mistress, who'd been
a mousy thing from the beginning

and no doubt made mousier
by his baseness. Still, he made
a show of mourning her, tattooing

rhododendrons on his head.
His wife had known
of the affair; a woman knows

that if she's getting kicked
a little less, someone else
is getting hers: a blessing

and a curse. And when Hope
dies she can't but miss her,
feeling sorry and complicit.

Annulment

We had to go back
to the beginning
to find a reason
why the marriage
never took, and
there it was, rooted
in the garden where
we mouthed our vows
beneath a prop plane
rented by old flames.
The plane circled noisily
above, our exes
yelling: *Don't*, and
Do me instead,
a ruckus that meant
we never really heard
the justice of the peace
or what we promised.
It turns out my mate
was saying: I'll love you
until intermission.
I swore: I'll darn
your socks until I don't.
Our past loves up
in the prop plane
could see the mistake
we were making.
If only they'd chosen
a helicopter, hovering
low enough to blow
fresh air into our brains,
we might have called it
quits before beginning.
But weddings happen
and unhappen, and my
unbethrothed and I
live happily un-after.

Garnish

Parsley sprig or melon
wedge next to the fried eggs.
Someone says: hold

the garnish, it's a waste,
and the waitress
refuses to serve him.

As if the kiss
at the nape
of the neck

could be loaded
onto scales, could
be weighed and measured.

Explication of Text

I heard you texted
John about the moon
last night. He gloated
when he told me.
I told him, no,
you didn't text me.
Why text the one
you're standing next to,
beneath that lucid moon?
Of course, there was
no moon last night,
none that could be seen.
It was like the way
you stood by me,
beyond what the naked
eye can glean. I read
between the lines,
between the clouds,
that's how, despite
facts to the contrary,
I found you,
breathless, there.

Sometimes I Drink Alone

The light is a very good
year: 2009. It's been aging
for ages. I drink it.
I drink it with a beautiful
woman, with a wood
nymph, with a faun. I say:
drink up, don't save a drop.
I've got another delivery
coming tomorrow. I buy
the stuff by the crate,
by the lot. It's
a lot to drink, a lot
to drink in. But if you
don't, it's gone, it sinks
into the sea, into easy
chairs, into seasoned valises.
This is a very good
year for light,
with just the right
hint of darkness.
Come in, but don't
sip. Guzzle.
It makes me
giddy, light–
headed to drink it,
to fall asleep drinking
it in and to wake
with back-orders of more
magnums piled high
beside the bed.

Transport

Don't expect a girl from Teaneck, New Jersey,
to show you everything, but Lena Lowenthal
showed me how to board a train in Baden-Baden
with a forged rail pass, how to keep riding

and not look back. The trick isn't in the ink, it's
not in the solvent used to lift a stranger's
name and date from the paper. The trick
is handing the ticket to the conductor while

staring long and hard at his loins, as if these were
the homeland you loved and were leaving forever.
It's what Lena's mother learned from her mother,
who tucked her in 1940 into the Black Forest,

into a train alone beneath a black
and star-starved sky, her own yellow
star torn off and burned, her mother
somewhere back there, not waving, burning.

The Gates of Paradise

The Gates of Paradise
are bitter, my father says.
Don't tell Francesca.
He doesn't mean to seem
ungrateful, tasting what he thought
he shouldn't—the dark
chocolate replica she's made
of a portion of Ghiberti's gates,
a one-off of the wax sculpture
she cast to better understand
how he made his masterpiece.
He wants to keep the cocoa
facsimile with the family
photos on the mantle, but I tell him
the chocolate won't last, the butter
will separate, the deep mahogany
mottle. Reluctantly, he breaks
off a bit with a boy and his dog.
This could be my Rex and me,
my father says, meaning he's nibbling
his childhood, which bears some
resemblance to the Gates of Paradise,
leading, as it did, to much contentment and many
letters to the editor. If he'd been
a more spiritual man, he'd have petitioned
his god. Instead, it's the editors,
to whom he offers suggestions,
which are different from complaint.
He sees a place as it one day may be.
He repeats: the Gates of Paradise are bitter,
handing me a brittle piece. It's the evening
of his eightieth birthday, a day
he held an open house that my mother
describes as a sort of happy wake,

the guest of honor serving barbeque.
The party's over. We're
the afterglow—insatiable,
devouring the Gates of Paradise
in the fleeting umber light we
seem to cast. Oh, they
are bitter, and we cannot stop.

Truth in Advertising

If we'd moved her,
she'd still have 'em,

the ad for Acme
Moving says, with a photo

of Venus de Milo.
But who, intact,

would Venus be?
Some standard-issue

ingénue. Give me
a woman who's lived

a little, who's wrapped
her arms around the ages

and come up lacking: that's
the stone that can move me.

Self Portrait with the Cinnabons

The Cinnabon Indians prefer
to be addressed as the Cinnabon
Native Americans. Any fool knows this.
What's that? Oh, mille apologia.
I misheard. It's the Assiniboine tribe
of Montana, not at all related
to the Cinnabon peoples who sell us
sticky buns we love in airports, those
fat-laden frosted squares
we wouldn't touch elsewhere.
But the limbo of airports permits
such reckless decadence. Dough
treats seem tame compared with the dangers
of lift-off and landing, so we allow
ourselves the sugar coma,
the rush associated with high-
risk ventures such as love
or lust, which are never far
from any terminal. If you're old enough,
you'll remember walking your beloved
to the gate, across the tarmac, even onto the plane.
Back then, you could step from Cincinnati
into the waiting room at O'Hare and never know
who might greet you. This was before the rise
of the Cinnabon people, who thrive
on our appetites for yeasty sweets, which
may have increased with tighter security measures.
The Assiniboine remember when everything
changed, how that happened slowly and all
of a sudden, and then from the spirit
of the U.S. government came Schlitz
in crushable cans and trailers
and the rez, where not much changed.
If you were a plains Indian

in Montana, you could lose everything,
you could lose your shirt, but
you'd still have your hair, and if
you're Assiniboine and you tell anybody,
hey man, you're beautiful, you mean
his hair, her hair. If you get
very close to someone, if
he trusts you, he'll let you
brush his hair, which he never
cuts, outside the trailer, or inside of it.
And if you're Assiniboine or Gros Ventre,
or anybody else for that matter,
you'll have to put your hair in netting
if you work in the Cinnabon.
It's hygienic and the law.
And if you're Assiniboine, there's
another advantage, since they believe
that if you haven't lead a righteous life,
when you die, you have to gather
all the hair you ever lost
on earth and burn it.
That's a real limbo for you,
a bonafide purgatory. I saved
a plastic sack of my own hair
clippings for no good reason
and peek in at the chestnut
and graying locks. They resemble
a delicate invertebrate which the remorseful
fingers of all my ex-loves
might like to pet. The sack of hair
is like a creature who used
to travel the world, downing
Cinnabons as if there were
no Cincinnati, no tomorrow, but who
no longer gets out much. If I
get my DNA tested, I may find
links to the Cinnabons or the Assiniboines,

but in the end, identity is a matter
of splitting hairs, isn't it?
It all comes down to having
someone you trust enough to comb
your infinite tresses or shine your bald pate.
When you get to the pearly gates
or whatever version of that
your faith allows, there may
or may not be a Cinnabon stand there.
They may or may not offer you a job
as a management trainee. If they do,
take it. Everything in life
and death is temporary: beauty,
the icing on the cake, the voice
over the loud speaker that says
the ground time, while brief, permits
a swift dash to the Cinnabon stand,
which for a limited time only,
in lieu of cash will take as payment
the wisdom of the Assiniboines
and one nomadic lock of hair.

Christmas Day, My 23rd Year

She's standing at the pay phone
outside the darkened Bartley's Burgers, snow
coming down, the street deserted, save
me headed to *Fool for Love*
and whoever was a dime away
inside that phone. Please, she says,
calling out. Tell me, am I
hideous to look at? I glance
at her quickly, afraid of what I'll see.
Then she turns slowly, as if
showing off a new dress.
I expect a gash or scar.
Instead I see the kind of woman
one walks past—
pale, middle-aged, widening,
what we call nondescript.
People walk past as if they couldn't
look at me, she says. You're not
hideous, I say, and then, unable
to stop my mother's cliché: it's what's
inside that matters. Do you want
to see what's inside me? she asks.
I stammer: I do, but I'm late.
Weren't you going to call someone?
I was, she says. But I need a dime.
I give her a dime.
I need a phone number, she says.
Someone to call. I give her
my number, with two or three digits
inverted. The movie turns out
to be twisted, sad, and brutal, and it's
only much later, when I don't
even recognize myself that I realize
the woman was my mother, who
had always asked for so little.

Kentucky Derby

Next year in Jerusalem,
with mint juleps. This year
in Peterborough, with Wyatt and Anna,
arriving at Brady's Sports Bar one minute
before the two-minute event begins.
In my minute, I circle the oval
faux-oak bar slowly, scanning for someone
I know. I say *hello*, people
make space for me and bring
a very cold beer. Anna says:
*I would not like to get in those
small spaces*, meaning whatever you call
the starting pens. Wyatt sizes me up
the way jockeys do. Full disclosure:
I'm too big to ride, too small
to amount to anything big. Then
they're off to the races: a muck-up
at the start, par for the course, and one
horse falls back. *Root for #12*, Anna says.
She likes 12 because his owner
won't dope him. *Go General Quarters*, I say.
The horses run. I am vaguely aware
of a recent tragedy in which the winning
horse stumbled, another in which many
horses succumbed to bad supplements.
There are other tragedies, of course, some
involving horses, some not, but we
won't delve into those. This is a two-
minute extravaganza and we're meant to focus
on the horses and the riders, not the men
in flannel caps, the men in their cups, howling
who-knows-what for who-knows-horse.
This is a moment to be in the moment and I
fail terribly, knowing nothing about

ponies, thinking: this is like a whirlwind
tour of abstract expressionism, which I don't
get because I don't get what was poured into it.
But my beer, confirmed on the second sip,
is exceedingly cold, with a taste of caramel and barrel,
and then someone wins the race, which sort
of means it's over and also just begun, since
now the replays start, with aerial shots
that show the winner. *Who's that, who's that?*
everyone asks, as the horse again swifts
from behind, finding his opening
the way any of us might
hope to, if the seas evaporated
on our behalf. And then the horse's name:
Mine that Bird, which seems strange, which
for me brings to mind the mynah bird my Uncle Joe
kept in a brass cage in Lipsitz Department Store
in Beaufort, South Carolina, a bird named Lippy whose two-
phrase repertoire included *Where's Joe?* and *Stride Rite,
Stride Rite*, the brand of shoe whose purchase
came with a plastic golden egg
filled with candies. What could be better?
Nothing, except the headline
of the obituary the day Lippy
the mynah bird died: Death
of a Salesman. I kid you not.
If Lippy were here in this bar, he'd
catch on quick, repeating *Mine
that Bird, Mine that Bird*. But
Lippy's not here. Instead, it's Wyatt
and Anna and me, and we agree, watching
the tiny, winning jockey sniffing
roses thrown his way, that as soon as he
dismounts the screen, he'll eat and eat
and eat, so he no longer resembles an Irish
Holocaust survivor grinning into the sunset.
I am going to eat too, I tell my friends.

I am heading back to my version of Eden, where
my days are numbered, but I'm fuzzy
on the number because sometimes fuzzy is easier,
and I'm a little fuzzy now, after half
a beer, reaching for the sweater on the back
of my bar stool. It's a white sweater, it's soft, and Anna
kindly reminds me that it is hers, and I leave
them, leave the sweater, and loop up the hill
toward corn bread, red beans and rice.
I'm late to mess, and someone pours me
a glass of Malbec, someone sits down next to me.
I'm being cared for as if I've been wounded,
which I suppose is the case, though I
don't want to know to what extent.
Someone says that once she was allowed
to choose a favorite food for dinner. Her sister
chose butter, she chose honey. We are all
made of honey and butter and one of us has a yellow
school bus which we board from time to time
for a field trip that involves riding in circles
and falling asleep, which involves
all of us being ponies in a meadow.
The sea and sky are made of grass.
It can't last. It lasts.

6

About the Author

ANDREA COHEN's poems and stories have appeared in *The Atlantic Monthly, Poetry, The Threepenny Review, Glimmertrain, The Hudson Review* and elsewhere. Her poetry collections include *The Cartographer's Vacation*, winner of the Owl Creek Poetry Prize, *Long Division* (Salmon, 2009), and *Kentucky Derby*. She has received a PEN Discovery Award, Glimmertrain's Short Fiction Award, and several residencies at The MacDowell Colony. She directs the Blacksmith House Poetry Series in Cambridge, MA.